Teaching, Parenting, and Mentoring Successful Black Males

A Quick Guide

Teaching, Parenting, and Mentoring Successful Black Males

A Quick Guide

MYCHAL WYNN

TEACHING, PARENTING, AND MENTORING SUCCESSFUL BLACK MALES: A QUICK GUIDE

ISBN-13: 978-1-880463-03-1
ISBN-10: 1-880463-03-2
Copyright © 2007 Mychal Wynn
Copyright © 2007 Rising Sun Publishing, Inc.
First Edition
Printing   1   2   3   4

The material contained in this book has been taken from the book, *Empowering African-American Males: A Guide to Increasing Black Male Achievement* covered under U.S. copyright by the author and publisher. All rights reserved. Any reproduction of material covered in this book without the expressed written permission from Rising Sun Publishing, Inc., is strictly prohibited except when quoted in brief reviews. No part of this book may be reproduced or transmitted in any form or by any means, electronic or mechanical, including photocopying, recording or storing in any information storage and retrieval system for commercial purposes.

Cover design and student photograph by Mychal Wynn.

Reference sources for style and usage: *The New York Public Library Writer's Guide to Style and Usage* copyright 1994 by The New York Public Library and the Stonesong Press, Inc., and the *APA Stylebook 2004* by the Associated Press.

Rising Sun Publishing, Inc.
P.O. Box 70906
Marietta, GA 30007-0906
770.518.0369/800.524.2813
FAX 770.587.0862
E-mail: info@rspublishing.com
Web site: http://www.rspublishing.com

Printed in the United States of America.

Acknowledgments

I would like to thank those parents, educators, counselors, and mentors who are championing Black male achievement and embracing the strategies outlined in the book, *Empowering African-American Males: A Guide to Increasing Black Male Achievement*, upon which this book is based. It is these champions who are turning the tide against seemingly insurmountable obstacles to help Black males experience school success as they discover their role in pursuing the American Dream.

Dedication

To my wife, for her patience, understanding, and support, and to our sons, Mychal-David and Jalani, who represent the promise and potential of Black males.

Table of Contents

About the Author		vii
Introduction		viii
Overview:	Why Focus on Black Males?	1
Chapter 1:	Mission	11
Chapter 2:	Vision	17
Chapter 3:	Climate and Culture	34
Chapter 4:	Curriculum and Content	71
Chapter 5:	Instruction	91
Chapter 6:	Assessment	97
Epilogue		111
What Manner of Men are We?		113
Reference		115
Index		116

About the Author

Mychal Wynn is an internationally-acclaimed author and educational consultant to school districts throughout the U.S., Canada, the Caribbean, and Bermuda. His life experiences—born into poverty in rural Pike County, Alabama; given up for adoption and raised in poverty amidst the gangs and violence in the Black urban ghetto of Chicago's South Side; an underachieving student and suspended from school throughout elementary and middle school; expelled from a Catholic high school and forced to attend one of the country's most violent public high schools where over 50 percent of the students dropped out and less than 10 percent went on to attend college—provides insight into, and an understanding of, the challenges confronting Black student achievement in general, and Black male achievement in particular.

Mychal Wynn and his wife, Nina, have successfully raised two sons, Mychal-David (currently attending Amherst College), and Jalani (currently attending middle school).

Introduction

This book provides a quick guide to the information contained in the book, *Empowering African-American Males: A Guide to Increasing Black Male Achievement [Wynn, 2005]*. Based on the book, data is presented, barriers are identified, and over 60 strategies are provided. As a parent, teacher, administrator, coach, counselor, mentor, law enforcement personnel, or concerned citizen, the strategies will direct your efforts in empowering and enabling more Black males to be successful in k-12 education and inspiring more of them to pursue postsecondary educational opportunities.

This book follows the school improvement/student achievement framework outlined in the book, *Increasing Student Achievement* (mission, vision, climate and culture, curriculum and content, instruction, and assessment). After reading this quick guide you may wish to refer to the entire text upon which this book is based for a more comprehensive set of strategies, data, reference sources, and discussion topics.

Introduction

Black males represent a demographically identifiable subgroup. They face unique barriers, require gender- and culturally-responsive strategies, and necessitate a specific focus within school communities to increase their levels of academic achievement, high school graduation, and college enrollment.

Overview

Why Focus on Black Males?

African-American Males—Black Males

While the title of the book upon which this quick guide is based *[Empowering African-American Males: A Guide to Increasing Black Male Achievement]* reflects the culturally appropriate term, "African-American" referring to Americans of African descent, the terminology, 'Black' will be used throughout the text. Whether Black American, Black Caribbean, Black Bermudian, Black Canadian, or Black African, the issues confronting Black males, and their parents, wherever they live, are very similar across cultural and socioeconomic lines. These boys, young men, and men who share a cultural frame of reference, are adversely influenced by peer pressures, frequently struggle in classrooms, are the students most likely to be disciplined, and are likely to matriculate through an educational system which fails to affirm their cultural contributions or connect them to their historical past. My mother, bless her soul, when told of my plans to visit Africa, asked, "Son, why are you going to Africa?" When I told her, "Mama, Nina and I are going on a tour of Egypt and Ghana to trace our roots," she responded, "Boy, you ain't from Africa; you were born in Alabama!"

African Black males, Bermudian Black males, Canadian Black males, Caribbean Black males, and Black males from Alabama face similar challenges in education, maturation, college matriculation, and, in gaining full access through the glass ceilings into the ivory towers of business in their respective countries, states, islands, and communities. Subsequently, the strategies set forth in this book, are pertinent to the raising, teaching, nurturing, and empowering of 'Black' males whether they live in the United States, Canada, Bermuda, Africa, or on one of the many islands in the Caribbean. Wherever they live, Black males suffer from a cultural disconnect in schools and classrooms. Hip-hop clothing, flashy jewelry, earrings, cornrows, brash language, body piercing, and tattoos further the cultural, gender, and generational divide.

1: identify the problem

Addressing the Black male crisis requires first, raising the question, "What is the problem?" If there is in fact a problem, we must raise the question, "What do we want to do about it?" The original version of the book, *Empowering African-American Males to Succeed: A Ten-Step Approach for Parents and Teachers [Wynn, 1992]*, cited the 1990 U.S. Census Bureau statistics:

African-American males have higher unemployment rates, lower labor force participation rates, lower high school graduation and college enrollment rates, while ranking first in incarceration and homicide as a percentage of the population.

The leading cause of death for African-American men between the ages of 15 and 24 is homicide. And, while representing only 6 percent of the population, African-American men represent 49 percent of prison inmates. Only 4 percent of African-American males attend college, while 23 percent of those of college age are either incarcerated or on probation. While African-American children nationwide comprise approximately 17 percent of all children in public schools, they represent 41 percent of all children in special education. Of the African-American children in special education, 85 percent are African-American males. African-American males, while comprising only 8 percent of public school students, represent the largest percentage, nationally, in suspensions (37 percent).

The tragic reality concerning the plight of Black males is, in the decade between the 1990 and 2000 census little changed. In many categories, the 2000 census shows a worsening of the Black male condition. As evidenced by data contained in the National Center for Education Statistics report, *Educational Achievement and Black-White Inequality,* there is no doubt there is a problem and something needs to be done about it.

2: focus on the data

Discipline, Special Education, and Jail

- Black students, while representing only 17 percent of public school students, account for 32 percent of suspensions and 30 percent of expulsions. In 1999, 35 percent of all Black students in grades 7-12 had been suspended or expelled from school. The rate was 20 percent for Hispanics and 15 percent for Whites.

- Black children are labeled "mentally retarded" nearly 300 percent more than White children and only 8.4 percent of Black males are identified and enrolled in gifted and talented classes.

- Black males in their early 30s are twice as likely to have prison records (22 percent) than bachelor's degrees (12 percent).

- A Black male born in 1991 (today's middle school student) has a 29 percent chance of spending time in prison at some point in his life. The figure for Hispanic males is 16 percent, and for White males is 4 percent.

- Black males are imprisoned at a rate of 3,405 per 100,000 (3.4 percent); Hispanics at a rate of 1,231 per 100,000 (1.2 percent); and Whites at a rate of 465 per 100,000 (.465 percent).

High School Performance

- Only 30 percent of Black high school students take advanced mathematics courses.

- Only 27 percent of Black high school students take advanced English.

- Only 12 percent of Black high school students take science classes as high as chemistry and physics.

- Only 5 percent of Black high school students take a fourth year of a foreign language with only 2 percent taking an AP foreign language course.

- Black students take AP exams at a rate of 53 per 1,000 students. The rate for Hispanic students is 115 per 1,000 and for Whites it is 185 per 1,000.

- The average ACT score for Black students is 16.9; for Whites it is nearly 30 percent higher at 21.8.

Unemployment

- 13 percent of Blacks ages 16-24 have not earned a high school credential.

- The unemployment rate for Blacks without a high school credential is 30 percent, 19 percent with high school but no college, 10 percent with some college but no degree, and 6 percent with a bachelor's degree.

While these statistics may be alarming for the general population, they have left barely any Black family untouched and place all Black males at risk. Societal perceptions, law enforcement interactions, and peer pressures of friends, relatives, and friends of friends who are either undereducated, unemployed, in gangs, involved in criminal activity, or on parole have an immediate and far-reaching impact on the lives of current and future generations of Black males. The issue for the Black community—indeed, for America—is much more than merely closing an achievement gap; it is ensuring that future generations of Black men have jobs, function as fathers, and contribute to the health and economic well-being of their local and national community.

3: build partnerships

It Takes A Village

Increasing Black male achievement will require a systemic and sustained collaboration between adults throughout the school community—the village. In the case of our sons, their academic and social development, school and personal success, exposure and opportunities, and maturation and spiritual development have been, and continue to be, the result of the village. A diverse group of stakeholders must be included in the discussion of problems, identification of solutions, and acceptance of roles in implementing strategies:

1. *Parents* must be actively involved in the academic, social, spiritual, and physical development of their sons and provide a household culture built around a set of spiritual core values and academic expectations that encourage and celebrate excellence.

2. *Teachers* must be willing to better understand the needs of parents, learning-styles of children, and have a genuine desire to ensure frequent opportunities for Black males to be successful in their classrooms.

3. *Counselors and Coaches* must be willing to supplement the lack of student/family knowledge in regards to academic planning, school success, and postsecondary preparation.

4. *Administrative leadership* must be willing to provide advocacy for Black males within their schools and programs and must encourage and expose students to a wide range of personal, intellectual, and artistic development opportunities.

5. *School-based support personnel*, i.e., custodians, law enforcement personnel, front office staff, and other non-instructional and administrative personnel must be willing to assume an active role in protecting, encouraging, and nurturing Black males throughout elementary, middle, high school, and college.

6. *Faith-based institutions* must understand and serve the needs of families and support the efforts of their local schools.

4: teacher collaboration

Teacher collaboration is crucial to the success of the village. Black male achievement cannot be viewed as a "sprint"—school opens, teachers distribute their syllabi, tell parents and students what their expectations are, and fail those students who do not run THEIR race at THEIR pace from the opening bell. Teaching and nurturing Black males through their own self-imposed obstacles and behaviors is a marathon—parents share what they know about their son's needs, teachers share their expectations, and *together* they devise strategies to meet student needs. This collaboration recognizes that one young man's pace throughout the race may not be at the same speed as other classmates. Oftentimes, males simply do not get out of the starting blocks as quickly as teachers or parents would like, or expect them to.

Chapter 1

Mission

Before forging ahead with assessing problems, conceptualizing solutions, or developing implementation plans, we must engage in the painstaking task of clarifying the mission, i.e., purpose. Contemplating, conceptualizing, and clarifying the mission is a time-consuming, self-reflecting, and gut-wrenching task that cannot be avoided. Consider the following questions within the context of the data previously presented:

- Who has the mission of increasing Black male enrollment in gifted, honors, higher-level mathematics, and AP classes?
- Who has the mission of increasing Black male high school graduation and college matriculation?
- Who has the mission of reducing Black male suspensions and increasing SAT and ACT scores?

Looking beyond the data, the question may be raised:

- What type of men do we want to develop and what level of achievement do we want these young men to strive for?

5: state the mission

A clear mission, guides and focuses our efforts. Without one, we are unlikely to identify, conceptualize, or implement the types of self-sustaining systems and programs necessary for substantive, systemic, and long-term changes in personal achievement and character development of Black males. We are more likely to experience a great deal of confusion, high level of personal anxiety, and seek comfort in resolving that their success, or lack thereof, is outside of our control: "I don't know what to do with these boys today. We've tried everything and nothing seems to be working."

The *Successful Texas School-wide Programs* research study noted:

These schools did not simply have Mission Statements, their sense of mission was articulated in every aspect of their planning, organization, and use of resources. Almost every decision about the selection of instructional materials; staff development; use of resources; scheduling of the school calendar; assignment of teachers, support personnel, and volunteers; and use of space was guided by a focus on the mission of ensuring the academic success of every student.

A clear and focused mission is also noted as one of the seven correlates identified in *Effective Schools* research:

- *Safe and Orderly Environment*
- *Climate of High Expectations for Success*
- *Instructional Leadership*
- ***Clear and Focused Mission***
- *Opportunity to Learn and Student Time on Task*
- *Frequent Monitoring of Student Progress*
- *Home–School Relations*

6: identify your role

There are many roles that you may choose to accept, each with unique opportunities to influence the lives of young men. While some roles are seemingly well defined—parent, teacher, counselor, coach, principal, pastor, or police officer—rarely will a single role suffice. Parents are forced to be teachers, teachers to be parents, coaches to be counselors, counselors to be psychologists, and all to be investigators! However, having a clear sense of the roles that you will or may play will define the sphere of your potential influence.

7: understand your influence

In each of your respective roles you will have varying levels of influence within the lives of Black males. Whether they are students in a classroom, children in your household, players on a team, students sent to the office, or young men standing before judges in courtrooms, you will have many opportunities to influence their lives. The character you model, language you use, lessons you convey, advice you impart, guidance you provide, and compassion you demonstrate will all influence the attitudes, behaviors, dreams and aspirations of Black males within your sphere of influence.

8: clarify your personal mission

Beyond the school or department's mission, what is your personal mission? What level of Black male achievement would you like for your role and influence to impact? Clarifying your personal mission will guide your efforts, frame your beliefs, and determine the breath and depth of the relationships you develop with colleagues, other adults, and the young people within your sphere of influence.

9: build relationships

Identify the relationships that are needed to pursue the mission.

Chapter 2

Vision

Taking the time to clarify your role, identifying the level of influence you want, and stating your mission must now be translated into a vision, i.e., what must be done to fulfill the mission. Conceptualizing a vision for your classroom, household, school, program, or church will require discussions with, and input from, the stakeholders who impact and influence the lives of the young men within your community. A shared vision by parents, teachers, coaches, counselors, and law enforcement personnel will translate into shared goals and common strategies. To assess your vision, check the boxes on the following page reflecting your focus.

1. Academic focus: ❑ proficiency ❑ advanced ❑ Gifted ❑ equity

2. Academic encouragement:
   ❑ passing to next grade ❑ qualifying for Honor Roll

3. Academic level of course work being inspired toward:
   ❑ On Level ❑ Gifted ❑ Honors ❑ AP ❑ Joint Enrollment

4. Overall educational focus:
   ❑ elementary ❑ middle school ❑ high school ❑ college

5. Extracurricular activity focus: ❑ Athletics ❑ Band
   ❑ Student Government ❑ Honor Society ❑ Beta Club

6. Talents and abilities being nurtured: ❑ Leadership ❑ Athletic
   ❑ Artistic/Creative ❑ Mathematic/Scientific ❑ Entrepreneurship

7. Summer programs being affirmed:
   ❑ Summer school ❑ Pre-College ❑ Leadership ❑ Athletic
   ❑ Academic enrichment ❑ Artistic/Creative ❑ None

8. Postsecondary focus:
   ❑ Trade/Technical ❑ Community College ❑ HBCU
   ❑ State University ❑ Elite University ❑ None

9. Career focus: ❑ Entry Level ❑ Trade ❑ Professional
   ❑ Manager/Executive ❑ Athlete ❑ Entertainer ❑ Entrepreneur

10: clarify your vision

Beliefs + Experiences = What You Do

Your beliefs and your experiences have already determined the focus of your mission and now, your beliefs will be more fully revealed through the scope of your vision. The vision that you affirm will provide focus and direction—it will frame your discussions (i.e., college and careers), guide your actions (i.e., providing enrichment opportunities, social exposure, and mentoring), and be reflected in the goals you establish (i.e., honor roll, Beta Club, college admission). The scope of your vision will influence the consciousness, beliefs, and goals that the young men whom you are focusing on set for themselves. The scope of their long-term dreams and the decisions reflected in their daily choices will be undeniably influenced by your vision.

11: clarify your beliefs

Purposefully lifting Black males to higher academic and personal achievement levels is a walk of faith many are simply unprepared, unwilling, or unable to take. They are bound by the limitations of their own beliefs.

- Few would disbelieve a Black male breaking 11 seconds in a 100-meter dash but could those same people believe in his breaking 30 on the ACT or 700 on each component of the SAT?

- Few would disbelieve a Black male running 100 yards in a football game but could those same people believe in his taking all honors and AP classes during any given school year?

Revisit your mission. Was it conceptualized with a focus on student/family deficits (e.g., below grade level, lack of preexisting knowledge, frequent discipline problems, lack of parental support, family living in poverty), or on your capacity (e.g., master motivator, believer in divine intervention, confident in your ability to identify people who will support your efforts, expert in teaching, parenting, counseling, or coaching)?

12: clarify your focus

According to the data, many Black males are living in poverty, being raised in single-parent households, and are below grade-level in one or more academic areas. Clarifying your focus will determine whether you are focused on:

- their deficits or your capacity;
- their inability or your ability;
- their foolishness or your wisdom;
- their childishness or your maturity; or
- their lack of knowledge or your wealth of knowledge.

13: focus your conversations

- Will your conversations focus on high school graduation or college matriculation?
- Will your academic support focus on getting A's, B's, or passing?
- Will you talk to them about reaching proficiency or reaching potential?
- Will you encourage their dreams and aspirations or will you try to assess what is "realistic?"
- Will you encourage them to take the most academically-challenging courses or suggest easy or remedial classes?
- Will you allow them to answer questions in single-word responses, i.e., "fine" or will you encourage them to speak in clearly distinguishable complete sentences, i.e., "I feel very well today, thank you for asking?"
- Will you allow them to submit inferior work or will you encourage them to strive for a higher standard?

14: inspire hope

Coach Ken Carter, former basketball coach at Richmond High School in Richmond, California, joins the list of educators to have had their vision of the promise and potential of young people portrayed in a movie:

- *The George McKenna Story*
- *The Marva Collins Story*
- *The Ron Clark Story*
- *Lean on Me (Joe Clark)*
- *Coach Carter*

The common thread woven through each story, was a vision, by a coach, principal, or teacher that more was possible for their students and that the history of low achievement, seemingly etched in stone, and accepted by adults and students alike, could be changed. Each person envisioned a level of achievement so far beyond the imaginations of those around them, their principal antagonists were adults, as opposed to the students themselves. Yet, in each situation, their vision inspired hope in their students and players. Coach Ken Carter envisioned a level of achievement in his players off of the basketball court that others could neither understand nor appreciate. His energy, strategies, language, stories, lessons, and expectations were all driven by his vision of a level of achievement, determined not by *their* circumstances or even *their* personal commitment, but by *his* experiences and *his* personal commitment. Only by convincing the young men of his commitment was he able to convince them of their potential. His vision, enabled him to develop the relationships and cultivate the culture needed to lead his players to internalizing this higher level of expectations. Once young men buy in to your vision and embrace your expectations, they are ready to combine their effort with your guidance. Coach Carter's players not only accepted his vision and embraced his expectations, they developed a level of intrinsic motivation that led them to pursue academic

Los Angeles Times, 2001
John M. Glionna

Coach Ken Carter, coach of the 13-0 Richmond High School basketball team, benched his entire 45-player roster on the varsity, junior varsity and freshman squads. He forfeited the next two league games and made the school gym off-limits even for practice. The entire team was benched until players raised their grades.

Coach Carter was quoted as saying, "On the streets and public basketball courts in Richmond and any other city in America, you see the broken dreams of former high school legends who got left behind by life. I was not going to let that happen to these boys."

In 1999, all 15 graduating seniors went on to attend four-year universities or junior colleges.

Coach Carter's tough-school philosophy didn't stop at the lockout. His players—many of whom were from low-income families and whom had never traveled the 10 miles from Richmond to San Francisco—began going on regular field trips to meet with investment bankers and other icons of the business world.

Although his most recent team finished a disappointing 6-13, Coach Carter and his players have their eyes set on a higher prize.

achievement with the same passion and commitment as they had previously pursued dunks, cross-over dribbles, and jump shots.

15: affirm your expectations

Adults within school communities have great power over the lives of children. From bus drivers to classroom teachers, from custodians to front office staff, from counselors to coaches, and from the principal to the safety officer—adults within each school community have enormous power to shape, and oftentimes save, the lives of young people.

The struggle with expectations is continual and undeniable. As young men challenge our authority, behave irresponsibly, are rude and ill-mannered, are dishonest, and demonstrate any number of confrontational or anti-social behaviors, we are challenged to believe in our capacity and in their potential. Their behaviors are not their burden as much as they are ours. We are the ones challenged with remaining steadfast, keeping our focus, and maintaining our perspective.

16: know their dreams

Knowing the dreams and aspirations of young men provides an important bridge of communication. What they want to achieve, where they want to go, and the changes they want to affect in their homes and communities all provide the opportunity to engage in meaningfully relevant dialogue about their current attitudes and behaviors. The fact that many young men have dreams and aspirations of pursuing careers in professional sports provides an invaluable opportunity to place discussions pertaining to current academic performance and college enrollment into the context of long-term goals that they are already affirming for themselves.

17: talk about their dreams

The book, *Follow Your Dreams: Lessons That I Learned in School [Wynn, 2000],* is an excellent tool for engaging young men in discussions about their dreams, the impact of peer pressure, and what is required to move beyond 'talking' about their dreams to actually putting forth the effort required to achieve their dreams.

Whenever a young man affirms a future, e.g., "I would like to become an attorney," we should use his aspiration as a springboard to affirming higher expectations. Presenting him with a book or magazine article about noted Black attorneys such as Thurgood Marshall, Johnnie Cochran, or Willie Gary; or assigning a research project on the National Bar Association, historical cases, or current issues before the Supreme Court may be used to nurture his interest, develop important academic skills, and expand his dreams.

"So you want to become an attorney. Let me tell you about Willie Gary ..."

Willie Gary was born in 1947, in South Georgia, the sixth of 11 children. The family lived in shacks. No shoes. Nothing.

After graduating from the Historically Black College, Shaw University, and within two years of opening his Stuart law firm, Willie Gary was a millionaire. He made national news when he reached a settlement of more than 40 million dollars with Florida Power & Light over the 1985 electrocution of seven rural Palm Beach County Florida residents.

His firm employs 150 people, including 21 lawyers, eight partners, two investigators, dozens of paralegals, a medical director and a public relations specialist. It represents more than 7,000 clients, including two groups of more than 2,000.

The 100 largest U.S. law firms average 400 million dollars in revenues, employ an average of 450 lawyers and generate about 500,000 thousand dollars per year in profits for the partners, according to the American Law Journal. Gary's firm generates almost 3 million dollars per lawyer in gross revenues.

Chapter 2: Vision

18: affirm college

Much more can be done to inspire and encourage Black males to aspire toward college. Once having inspired them, teachers, parents, coaches, and counselors must create the support mechanisms to prepare them to succeed in academically rigorous classes. The doorway to college may be opened as a result of their athletic, artistic, musical, dramatic, dance, or academic abilities. This is why early identification and nurturing of each young man's unique talents and gifts is critically important. Our older son's way to college began with his first-grade passion for art. Our younger son's fifth-grade talent in acting may become one of the special attributes that paves the way for his college admission. However, it is academically rigorous course work that will help them to succeed once they get there.

19: affirm higher-level math

According to the U.S. Department of Education's data, if young men are encouraged to pursue math beyond algebra I and geometry, they are substantially more likely to attend college. A vision of college-level achievement will directly impact the level of planning by parents and encouragement and intervention by school personnel.

The U.S. Department of Education's white paper, *Mathematics Equals Opportunity*, examined the impact of middle school math and science classes on college enrollment through a National Education Longitudinal Study of 26,000 public and private school 8th-grade students from 1988 through 1996. The report found that low-income students who take algebra I and geometry are almost 300 percent more likely to attend college as those who do not.

- 83 percent of all students (71 percent of low-income students) who take algebra I and geometry go on to college within two years of their scheduled high school graduation while only 36 percent of all students (27 percent of low-income students) who do not take algebra I and geometry courses go on to college.
- 60 percent of students who take calculus in high school took algebra in the eighth grade.

20: discuss college early and often

The study further determined, enrollment in gatekeeper courses, such as algebra I and foreign language, in eighth grade helps students reach higher levels in the mathematics and foreign language pipelines. For example, students who enroll in algebra I as eighth-graders are more likely to reach higher-level math courses (i.e., algebra III, trigonometry, or calculus) in high school than students who do not enroll in algebra I as eighth-graders.

According to the National Center for Education Statistics:

- Only 31 percent of Blacks ages 18-24 are enrolled in college while the percentage for Whites is 68 percent.
- Only 37 percent of Black college students are male.

21: use visual imagery

Parents can reinforce the college-bound message by replacing some of their son's FUBU, Phat Farm, Sean John, and other hip-hop shirts with college T-shirts and their NBA and NFL jerseys with college jerseys. Young men can be encouraged to adorn the T-shirts representing their favorite entertainer's alma mater. (Sean "P. Diddy" Combs attended Howard University.)

Students should be encouraged to write letters to colleges and universities asking for view books, catalogs, admission applications, pennant flags, T-shirts, and posters as a means of creating college-bound walls throughout their school.

Schools can host college T-shirt days, teachers can decorate walls within their classrooms with paraphernalia from their alma mater, classrooms can be named after colleges, corridors can be renamed to "College Lane, University Avenue, Ivy League Court, HBCU Boulevard, etc.," and display cases and bulletin boards can reflect college facts and information. There are many opportunities to discuss a student's college-bound dreams, connect a student's interests to college-level study, and continually reinforce academic performance, class selection, and standardized test scores within the context of meeting college admissions standards.

Chapter 3
Climate and Culture

Understanding the unique issues (i.e., media images, peer pressures, societal perceptions, and cultural icons) influencing the attitudes and behaviors of Black males is needed to develop effective communication, intervention, and empowerment strategies. The level of consciousness demonstrated by many Black males, is perhaps best articulated by Carter G. Woodson, in *The Mis-Education of the Negro*:

When you control a man's thinking you do not have to worry about his actions. You do not have to tell him not to stand here or go yonder. He will find his 'proper place' and will stay in it. You do not need to send him to the back door. He will go without being told. In fact, if there is no back door, he will cut one for his special benefit.

The over representation of Black males in special education, on athletic teams, and in suspensions, together with their under representation in gifted programs, on the school's honor roll, and in college matriculation shapes attitudes and beliefs within every school community.

22: compassion-yes; pity-no!

A sincere desire to understand the issues confronting Black males requires our compassion. However, the sociocultural influences, that continually shape Black male culture, do not necessitate our pity. Black males need teachers who will teach them, parents who will raise them, and adults throughout the school community who are willing to acknowledge the unique issues confronting them in discussing and developing strategies to empower them.

23: agree on expectations

Teachers and parents have to join forces and agree on expectations. Parents and teachers can only arrive at this point of agreement if they take the time to clarify their missions and visions. Teachers who associate pity with providing an opportunity for a student to turn in a late assignment or retake a test do not understand his needs, the family's needs, or the mission—teaching and learning. Consider, if a 500-word paper is due on Monday, the teacher could require a 700-word paper on Tuesday, a 900-word paper on Wednesday, or a 2000-word paper if turned in anytime prior to the end of the grading period. Failing test grades should be unacceptable. Retests should be mandatory until the desired level of content knowledge is achieved.

The consequence of late work or failing test grades should be more work. Zeroes do not inspire young men to do more work nor does an 'F' on a test inspire more study. If they do not care about their grades it does not even punish them—it punishes their parents! In this day of state and federal school accountability mandates, it ultimately punishes the school. If the assignment was meaningful to begin with, then the important concern is stimulating the intrinsic desire to do the work, and providing every opportunity for the student to put forth the effort to acquire the knowledge.

24: coach for success

There is much that parents and teachers can learn from coaches, who are oftentimes great motivators of young men, i.e., mental preparation, communication, motivation, respect, high expectations, providing frequent opportunities to succeed, and most importantly, developing a relationship where young people want to work for you.

A math teacher who 'coaches' student achievement may engage in the following encounter:

"Mr. Johnson, you got a '65' on the test. See me after school in three days for a retest!"

"Mr. Johnson, you got a '75' on the retest. See me after school in three days for another retest."

"Mr. Johnson, you got an '85' on the second retest. See me after school in three days for another retest."

"Mr. Johnson, you got a '95' on the third retest. I guess we have resolved that you are an 'A+' student. Let's try to be an 'A+' student on the first test next time."

Another math teacher stops at the first test and says, "Mr. Johnson you should have studied. You had better study harder the next time or you are going to fail the class." When is the young man going to learn what was not understood during the first test? Who knows what type of personal challenges he is confronting in his life, if there is a teaching-style–learning-style mismatch, if the young man lacks the preexisting knowledge, or if he simply needs more opportunities to 'get it.' Isn't 'getting it' the real goal?

More work increases learning, a failing grade merely punishes a young man for an entirely foreseeable event—poor test preparation, misplaced homework, late papers and projects. Punishing them with low grades, berating them in front of their peers, referring them to the office, or forcing them to spend long hours in detention does not accomplish the primary goal, TEACHING THEM!

25: nurture learning

Nurturing learning requires that we strengthen the relationship between the teacher (classroom teacher, parent, mentor, coach, or counselor) and learner (student, player, mentee, or child).

Strong relationships:

- inspire trust;
- communicate caring and compassion;
- are based on mutual respect;
- establish a level of confidence that you (as the adult) can be depended upon; and
- establish you (as the teacher) as possessing knowledge, wisdom, experience, or some level of disciplinary expertise.

26: see the individual

Shed biases and discard stereotypes. When Black males walk into classrooms or onto athletic fields they must be assessed individually rather than as representative of some larger identifiable 'Black culture.'

To assess Black males individually:

- get to know them (i.e., personality type, learning-styles, multiple intelligences, strengths and weaknesses);

- visit their homes and get to know the hopes and dreams of their families;

- get to know the make-up of their family unit (i.e., single-parent, grand parents, only child, siblings, foster care, multiple generations within the household);

- get to know their peer group, peer culture, and peer values;

- get to know their hopes, dreams, and aspirations;

- get to know their heroes, heroines, and role models (i.e., parent, older sibling, teacher, coach, entertainer, athlete);

- understand their reputation without being unduly influenced by it (i.e., frequent office referrals or suspensions, loud talking teachers, confrontational attitudes);

- understand their level of preexisting knowledge (i.e., experiences outside of their community, cultural exposure);

- understand their socioeconomic frame of reference (i.e., living in poverty, homeless, middle class, affluent);

27: understand their influences

- understand their family exposure to postsecondary education and careers (i.e., the educational background and type of work their parents do);
- understand their experiences within the school setting (i.e., interactions with peers and other adults).

Getting to know the Black males within a school community requires a willingness to understand what has shaped their attitudes and behaviors and to accept that the influences may be contrary to the values, beliefs, and cultural frame of reference of their homes.

Beverly Daniel Tatum, in *Why Are All the Black Kids Sitting Together in the Cafeteria?* notes:

In <u>The Autobiography of Malcolm X</u>, as a junior high school student, Malcolm was a star. Despite the fact that he was separated from his family and living in a foster home, he was *an 'A' student and was elected president of his class. One day he had a conversation with his English teacher, whom he liked and respected, about his future career goals. Malcolm said that he wanted to be a lawyer. His teacher responded, 'That's no realistic goal for a nigger,' and advised him to consider carpentry instead. The message was clear: You are a Black male, your racial group membership matters, plan accordingly. Malcolm's emotional response was typical—anger, confusion, and alienation. He withdrew from his White classmates, stopped participating in class, and eventually left his predominately White Michigan home to live with his sister in Roxbury, a Black community in Boston.*

In regards to the impact of Black household culture on Black youth culture, Tatum notes:

In adolescence, as race becomes personally salient for Black youth, finding the answer to questions such as, 'What does it mean to be a young Black person? How should I act? What should I do?' is particularly important. And although Black fathers, mothers, aunts, and uncles may hold the answers by offering themselves as role models, they hold little appeal for most adolescents. The last thing many fourteen-year-olds want to do is to grow up to be like their parents. It is the peer group, the kids in the cafeteria, who hold the answers to these questions. They know how to be Black. They have absorbed the stereotypical images of Black youth in the popular culture and are reflecting those images in their self-presentation.

Because of powerful media forces [radio, television, video games, hip-hop culture] influencing the ways Black children speak, walk, dress, style their hair, and pierce and tattoo their bodies, we dare not dismiss such influences as "the times in which we live." To the contrary, we must recognize, realize, and conceptualize ways to limit a young person's exposure on the one hand and engage him or her in critical-thinking discussions on the other. Unfortunately, the curriculum is not as dynamic as the culture. The lyrics, music video imagery, advertisements, television sitcoms, talk shows, and news reports of the many exploits of the heroes and heroines of today's generation have to make their way into classroom discussions and critical-thinking analysis.

28: regulate media exposure

One of the most dangerous things parents can do is to leave their sons at home with a working television with a cable connection and a computer with Internet access. Equally as dangerous, is a young man, a television, and a computer, alone in a bedroom with the door closed. There is simply too much inappropriate content and too many predators. Far too many young men are below grade level in reading and math while they have a household full of video games, DVDs, and 24-7 television access. Parents have to stop blaming everyone for their son's attitude, behavior, and low academic performance and do a check-up from the neck-up! No child should be spending more time watching television or playing video games than he is reading, engaged in sports, or otherwise being engaged in mentally or physically stimulating activities.

29: be resilient

As adults, we must better understand the world of today's young people and not bury our heads in the sand. The only way that we, as adults, can know the images, language, and messages which young people are being exposed to is to listen to their music, watch their videos, watch the television programming they are watching, and visit the Internet web sites they are accessing.

Young people in general, and Black males in particular, need teachers who will teach and parents who will raise them. My wife and I are not perfect parents—as our sons will most certainly attest to—however, as parents, we have a God-given responsibility to do the best we can to counter-balance the values and images our sons are bombarded with through the media and from their peers.

As parents, my wife and I are resilient in our resolve to:

1. *Make education a priority in our household.* Rarely a day goes by without my wife and me asking our sons about school. Reading and schoolwork is tied to everything. You cannot go to the movies unless your schoolwork is done. You cannot play a video game unless you have read for the amount of time you intend to play the video game. Your weekend does not begin until your homework has been completed.

2. *Take control over the radio station.* Personally, I prefer to listen to the Tom Joyner Morning Show in the morning and old school programming throughout the rest of the day. While I give my sons some flexibility in changing the station they know when music is inappropriate and they are quick to change to another station.

3. *Regulate television and video games.* We eliminate television and video games from Sunday evening through Thursday evening during the school year.

4. *Regulate their clothes.* Our sons are allowed hip-hop fashions, but they have to wear a belt and my wife and I impose limits.

5. *Understand their interests.* Discussing the music, fashions, people, and images our sons are exposed to and interested in helps us to better understand their influences.

6. *Reinforce Standard English usage and discourage overuse of slang.* We consider overuse to represent when you do not know any other way to communicate, but through the use of slang.

7. *Carefully choose role models.* We do not promote actors, athletes, or entertainers as role models. We look for local heroes and heroines who reflect the values, character, and spirituality as we teach in our household.

8. *Not allow piercing or tattoos.* This is a decision that our sons can make when they are grown, on their own, and paying their own bills.

9. *Not reaffirm negative images.* We have never taken our sons to a Rap concert or to see a hip-hop artist who promotes sex or the 'N-word' in his or her music.

10. *Not affirm professional sports or entertainment as career aspirations.* This is not to suggest our sons could not pursue professional sports or entertainment if this is truly their dream, however, my wife and I do not affirm such aspirations as an alternative to an education or intellectual pursuits.

30: spend quality time together

All parents are challenged with counter-balancing the negative language, images, and ideas proliferating the airwaves, television programming, music videos, video games, and movies. Whether spending the day together at a Track and Field Meet or spending Spring Break and summer vacations together, strong families provide the best foundation from which to nurture and develop strong Black men.

31: spread their wings

The story of *The Eagles who Thought They were Chickens* provides an invaluable instructional lesson for teachers and discussion prompt for parents, mentors, counselors, and coaches. The posture young men display, level of self-respect and respect for authority they demonstrate, and language they use are reflected in the attitudes and behaviors of the eagles, chickens, and roosters in the story.

No matter what position you take in the debate pertaining to usage of the 'N-word,' words have power. In the Biblical book of *Ephesians* [4:29] it states,

Let no corrupt communication proceed out of your mouth, but that which is good to the use of edifying, that it may minister grace unto the hearers.

The dehumanizing language of 300 years ago, directed at the millions of Africans, kidnapped from their villages, shackled and taken aboard slave ships, and shipped throughout the Caribbean and the Americas is now embraced by the descendents of those Africans and used each day to denigrate the image of themselves and of their children. It is a common occurrence within classrooms, on athletic teams, and in Black households to hear young Black males referring to each other as 'niggers,' calling each other 'stupid,' and affirming each other's failure, "You ain't gonna be nothing."

32: use language to affirm

When my wife and I were attending Crenshaw Christian Center, in Los Angeles, California, our pastor, Dr. Frederick K.C. Price, preached a sermon, "There is life-giving power in the power of the tongue." Through his message he referred to biblical scriptures that illustrated the spiritual power contained within the words, language, and thoughts conveyed by what we say.

Self-help gurus refer to this phenomenon through such axioms as, "Your attitude determines your altitude" or "You are what you say you are."

33: reinforce Standard English

The use of non-standard or non-conforming language patterns is common among many ethnic and geographical cultures. In Black culture, the use of non-Standard English is a bonding mechanism which utilizes culturally-appropriate language patterns and usage, i.e., "I ain't got none, ain't gon' be none, and don't won't none!" However, Standard English is the 'cash language.' It is what schools teach and the way that employees are expected to speak in a professional workplace. This is the language used by educators, professionals, and white-collar workers. The language educated Blacks learn to use, and most frequently, choose to use.

Non-Standard English is an undeniable communication mechanism that connects Blacks across socioeconomic, educational, and geographical boundaries, and enjoys a situational-appropriateness in the oratory of educated and well-spoken Blacks who masterfully use *code-switching* for emphasis during public oratory. However, young men must learn the standard before they can code-switch to what may be considered more culturally appropriate language patterns.

34: identify communication gaps

There are many communication gaps that we must identify and understand before we can overcome the cultural disconnect between adults and Black males:

- *Generational:* While some adults still behave like children, most adults will experience a generational gap between the values, ideas, language, expectations, attitudes, and behaviors between themselves and today's youth. The best way to address this gap, as with all other gaps, is through open and honest communication. Address the differences through critical-thinking, e.g., "That is an interesting style you have wearing your pants around your butt. Did you know that style was first popularized by prison inmates? I heard that men did it as a signal they were another man's girlfriend. What statement are you trying to make?" As opposed to an emotional response, e.g., "Boy, you and your friends are just ignorant!"

- *Gender:* If men are from Venus and women are from Mars, Black males are from the twilight zone. Women should anticipate misunderstandings and communication breakdowns.

- *Ethnic:* The fist thing for a non-Black teacher to openly acknowledge is the reality that he or she is not Black. The children know it so the teacher may as well admit it. Every ethnic group has a cultural frame of reference that can only be truly understood by those within the culture as is the case with gender differences.

- *Socioeconomic:* If you are not poor, read Ruby Payne's book, *A Framework for Understanding Poverty.* If you are poor, still read the book to better understand the needs of children living in poverty, particularly, the need they have to understand the 'Hidden Rules.' Oftentimes, it is their failure to fully understand the hidden rules as it relates to school behaviors, course enrollment, and college planning which hinders them in developing college-bound plans or even affirming college aspirations.

35: influence school culture

More than any other cultural variable, school culture represents the most powerful influence on the academic achievement of Black males. This is not to suggest that parents are absolved of their responsibility in nurturing the academic achievement of their sons, however, unless they choose to home school, their children spend more of their waking hours around adults within the school community—school bus drivers, support staff, classroom teachers, and coaches—than they do with parents during the school year. The academic foundation, values, and critical-thinking skills taught at home are either nurtured, expanded upon, or undermined during their son's many hours in school and their involvement in school-related activities.

As a result of the powerful cultural influence of schools, parents must learn how to identify, understand, and intervene when school culture is not nurturing of Black male academic achievement, social development, or college enrollment. Jawanza Kunjufu has coined the phrase, "The Conspiracy to Destroy Black Boys" in his series of books on the topic. Despite state accountability standards, Black male achievement task forces, and school improvement plans, many school communities cultivate the existence of such a conspiracy through their failure to recognize and respond to the cultural influences occurring within the school which are having a negative impact on Black male achievement. The reality of school culture is that it is either defined by adults, or by default, is defined by children. Either adults set the standards, define the boundaries, establish the values, create the appropriate customs and rituals, or by default, they are established by children.

Dr. Crystal Kuykendall in her keynote address before the Wholistic Institute tells the story of "Lying Lewis."

"In the seventh grade I had a student called 'Lying Lewis.' Everybody had warned me about Lewis. And when Lewis entered my classroom, I immediately knew that they were right! This boy could lie. And he was good too!

I started telling Lewis that anybody who knows intuitively what to say and make people believe it had a special gift.

I told Lewis that he would make a great politician! I wanted Lewis to know that there was a high road consistent with his special gifts.

Every time that I called on Lewis I would say, 'Assemblyman Hester, or Congressman Hester, or Senator Hester.' I would bring Lewis into the classroom discussions by saying, 'Senator Hester, do you have an opinion on this?'

It got to be so good to Lewis that he corrected me one day and said, 'Call me President Hester!'"

36: understand gender differences

Dr. Kuykendall discovered some years later, 'Lying Lewis' went on to become Attorney Lewis Hester. Dr. Kuykendall, by affirming potential where others had affirmed failure, put this young man on the high road of life!

In addition to the cross-cultural, socioeconomic, and generational issues influencing school culture, research pertaining to gender issues in schools and classrooms should be closely examined.

Michael Gurian, in *Boys and Girls Learn Differently: A Guide for Teachers and Parents,* notes:

- *Extracurricular Activities:* Girls make up the majority of student government officials, after-school club leaders, and school community liaisons.

- *Specific academic performance:* Girls are approximately one and a half years ahead of boys in reading and writing competency, according to statistics tracked by the Federal Department of Education.

- *Educational aspirations:* Colleges are 60 percent female. The Federal Department of Education has found that eighth-grade and twelfth-grade girls have, on average, higher educational aspirations than boys.

- *Learning and behavioral disorders:* Females are less likely to experience learning, psychiatric, or behavioral disorders. Boys make up two-thirds of the learning disabled and 90 percent of the behaviorally disabled, and nearly 100 percent of the most seriously disabled. Boys account for 80 percent of brain disorders.

- *Culture bias:* The educational system and the individual classroom are not as well designed for male brain development as for female. The system comprises mainly female teachers who have not received training in male brain development and performance; it relies on less kinesthetic, relatively monitored, and less disciplined educational strategies than many males need.

The socioeconomic, cultural, gender, and generational gaps contribute to parent-teacher misunderstandings, student-teacher confrontations, classroom disruptions, office referrals, in-school detentions, out-of-school suspensions, and, by all measures, unsatisfactory academic performance.

37: home-school communication

Janice Hale-Benson, in *Black Children: Their Roots, Culture, and Learning-styles*, notes the importance of establishing effective home-school communication and clear behavioral expectations:

> *The young child learns (probably very quickly because he has older children to help him) that adults in the school do not function in the same way that adults do in his community and that only behavior of gross impropriety (flunking, suspension) will be reported to his parents because school adults are not community agents of social control. He is free to act 'like he wouldn't act at home.'*

The lore of 'school readiness' suggests that children come to school socialized in such a fashion that the locus of social control has been internalized. Hence, teachers expect Black children to behave as 'good' children should (and good little White children do). It seems that the children and the teachers have mutually incompatible expectations of each other. Over a period of time, they tend to work out rather shaky adjustments to each other. The teachers conclude that the children are incorrigible, and the children conclude that the teachers are inconsistent and capricious.

38: practice the 4Cs

It is critical for parents and teachers to practice the 4Cs: Caring; Clarity; Commitment; and Consistency *[Ten Steps to Helping Your Child Succeed in School, p. 70]*. Caring about teaching and raising Black males, clearly defining the rules and consequences, remaining committed to reinforcing your behavioral expectations, and being consistent with both rewards and consequences establishes an effective classroom or home culture. Practicing these 4Cs, together with the following suggestions, can assist parents and teachers in establishing the foundation of discipline and respect.

1. Establish the rules and consequences early, enforce them regularly, and consider appending them when appropriate.

2. When you make a request and there is no immediate response, allow the benefit of the doubt and repeat yourself only to ensure that you were heard. Since new areas of behavior are always presenting themselves, it is not unreasonable to discuss why certain behavior is expected.

3. If your son (or student) is unresponsive or in any way fails to meet your expectations, enforce the previously established consequences.

39: teach 'value for value'

Establish chores at home or classroom expectations that bear a direct relationship to the things young men want, establishing a "value for value" relationship—value given for value received. Too many young men grow up believing they are entitled to something for nothing.

4. Learn to control your tone of voice. Frequently raising your voice implies you are not serious until you are screaming or threatening.

5. Do not discipline out of anger, discipline out of love. In your mind, you must clearly know why you are enforcing a certain consequence and you must stick to your decision. Do not confuse young men by constantly changing your mind. You have the responsibility to display leadership and enforce your authority.

6. Do not issue idle threats! Young men are not buying any "wolf tickets." If you are going to discipline, do so. If you are not, do not threaten.

7. Do not to speak to young men in a disrespectful way. The foundation of discipline and mutual respect must be established early, reinforced constantly, and modeled continually.

Na'im Akbar, in *Visions for Black Men*, describes the transition that boys undergo:

A male, a boy, and a man are not the same thing. A male is a biological creature, a boy is a creature in transition, and a man is something that has arrived to a purpose and a destiny. When men become real men and do not confuse their maleness or their boyishness with their manliness, they have come into a true rediscovery of what they are. There are problems with those who confuse their biological functions with their spiritual function as men. There are problems with 'boys' who think they're men—who enjoy playing games, who enjoy riding in fast cars, who enjoy listening to loud music, who enjoy running after women, and who enjoy running real fast rather than being steady and directed as men are.

Encouraging, allowing, and demanding that young men assume personal responsibilities will develop character, build self-esteem, and encourage self-directed behavior—it will prepare young Black men for a future of hope and promise.

Ron Weaver, in *Beyond Identify: Education and the Future Role of Black Americans*, states:

> *Several properties of classroom organization have been identified as important for development of a high degree of self-esteem in children. First, the children, especially minority children, must be afforded a sense of mastery—the degree to which they view themselves as able to manipulate events and achieve desired goals—over what happens to them in school. Through such mastery or decision-making opportunity, children may develop self-responsibility. This, in turn, may provide motivation in the sense that the children feel they, rather than someone else, are responsible for their success and failure. Subsequently, this role of self-direction may provide greater initiative in seeking success in school, since Black children's views of the environment of the school—how <u>open</u> and manipulable the environment seems to be—has been noted as more important to Black children than their competence in determining success.*

40: teach responsibility

George Henderson, in the same book, notes:

Studies in the foundations of humanistic education for Black students also indicate that Black students are better served when they have an active voice in the decision-making process which attends learning and accept the responsibility of the consummation of the decisions made. Indeed, self-concept and personal esteem are heightened when students share in their own educational development and emotional growth.

It is important for young Black men, to believe that they, rather than someone else, are primarily responsible for their success and failure—whether academic, social, personal, or professional. Black men who learn to approach the challenges and obstacles of life with the level of passion and intensity they demonstrate on basketball courts and football fields will be prepared to successfully fulfill their roles as husbands, fathers, and contributors.

41: make a connection

1. Consciously focus on "What can be" rather than "What you see." Always try to discuss current behaviors within a future context.

2. Familiarize yourself with the issues and images influencing the language and behaviors of Black males by reading the magazines and listening to the music young men listen to and take advantage of opportunities to talk to them about the images, advertisements, and influences.

3. Avoid lecturing and consciously look for opportunities to ask questions, solicit opinions, and stimulate their critical-thinking skills.

4. Develop a reservoir of stories, examples, and anecdotes that relate to the challenges, issues, and obstacles confronting young men.

5. Develop open communication with parents to share information, communicate consistent messages, and develop consistent strategies.

6. Develop a library of culturally relevant books and reading material.

7. Connect literacy to your circle of influence. A coach can prepare a reading list for players, a mentor can find books which relate to a young man's areas of interests and use them as a prompt to discuss ideas and interests, a teacher can add book reports to his or her list of extra credit opportunities.

8. Look for opportunities to identify other people to reinforce your message, i.e., athletes, entertainers, coaches, older young men, artists, poets, entrepreneurs, or others involved in work or careers that young men aspire toward.

9. Reinforce Standard English usage, respect for authority ("Yes sir, No Ma'am"), polite manners, and strong handshakes.

10. Be patient.

42: parenting is a full-time job

1. Develop household rules, expectations, rewards, and consequences with a future focus, i.e., father, husband, college graduate.

2. While you may be your son's friend you MUST be your son's parent.

3. Get involved with your son's school and influence his peer group through the booster club, tutorial program, or other volunteer opportunities.

4. Do not allow your son to go over to anyone's home prior to your having an opportunity to visit their home or know their parents.

5. Encourage your son to use correct grammar around you.

6. Do not allow your son to put clothes before learning. What is on his back (or feet) is not as important as what is between his ears!

7. Do not allow your son to disrespect adults, even if he believes he has been wronged. If you feel he has been wronged then you handle it. Adults should deal with adults.

8. Teach your son to keep his manhood to himself and not to make babies until he is married.

9. Do not allow your son to be a thug unless you are trying to raise a thug. If you are trying to raise a thug then you should go to church and allow someone to pray for you!

10. Do not have more DVDs, CDs, TVs, or video games in your home than books and control use of the media that you have!

11. Learn how to listen. Young men who are encouraged to talk will grow into men who have something to say. You will also discover that the longer a young man talks in an attempt to explain or to justify his actions, the more likely he is to "hear" just how ridiculous his actions were!

Chapter 4
Curriculum and Content

The area of curriculum and content encompasses many hotly debated issues that state departments of education, school boards, schools, and classroom teachers continually grapple with, i.e., content alignment between grade levels, content alignment with standardized or state testing, stereotypes and cultural bias in textbooks, the scope of interdisciplinary collaboration between content areas, and whether or not the breath and depth of the curriculum is appropriate. The intellectual and far-reaching nature of the debate on what, when, and how to teach is far too complex to be addressed within the scope of this book. The focus here will be to ensure that Black males are engaged in academic rigor and that Black families gain full access to whatever curriculum is being offered.

43: create a web of protection

The answer to the question, "Do Black males and their families fully understand the complete scope of curriculum offerings in the district, the importance of advanced science and math, the weight of honors and AP classes on GPA calculations, and how to construct college-bound plans to pursue student dreams and aspirations?" is NO! To ensure that Black males gain full access to the curriculum, are enrolled in academically rigorous classes, and develop comprehensive college-bound plans, a web of protection is needed to protect them against the negative influences of peers, low expectations of teachers, lack of encouragement of parents, and lack of confidence within themselves.

Creating a web or protection will require identifying:

1. The roles to be played, values to be conveyed and reinforce, and relationships to be developed.
2. The individuals and programs needed to provide the necessary information and support (i.e., school-based personnel, community involvement, athletic programs, neighbors, etc.).
3. The negative influences or counter-cultural values (e.g., devaluing of academic achievement).

44: reduce negative influences

The power of the media to influence the images that Black males have of themselves and the images that the society at-large has of Black males is undeniable. Typical of media imagery is:

- aggressiveness in walk, talk, and demeanor;
- use of profanity and combative behavior when confronting authority figures;
- sexual promiscuity, sexually explicit language, degradation of and violence toward women;
- idolization of intimidating clothing styles, use of tattoos, hand gestures, a confrontational mentality, and certain body images (e.g., hair, weight, body piercing);
- desensitizing of violent acts;
- association of alcohol and drug use with being cool;
- association of financial success with cars, motorcycles, jewelry, houses, and sex;
- use of violence as the primary means of resolving conflicts;
- association of fame and financial success with manhood and such success insulates a person from having to face the consequences of his actions; or
- defining opportunities for personal and financial success as largely limited to entertainment, professional athletics, and criminal activities—none of which require high levels of formal education.

Each of the media influences is exacerbated through the continual reinforcement among peers, who themselves have been influenced by media images and popular cultural norms and values. Peer pressure is exerted within the school community, on athletic teams, and through the daily formal and informal interactions between males. These pressures, to a great extent, influence attitudes and behaviors as males seek to conform and belong to peer groups.

45: choose your lessons

To effectively convey the messages and reinforce the needed values we must identify and use:

- lessons,
- stories,
- proverbs,
- parables,
- programs, and
- other adults.

Take advantage of every opportunity (i.e., dinner table discussions, classroom lessons, church sermons, etc.) to discuss the character values, leadership skills, and community consciousness that you envision young boys developing on their journey into manhood.

46: do not let TV raise your child

Television Programming: My wife and I limit the amount of time and access to television programming. We simply believe that if our sons are not 'A' students there is no time for television during the school year between Sunday evening and Thursday evening. In the case of our younger son, who *is* an 'A' student, between the amount of time devoted to after-school activities, e.g., martial arts, football, rehearsals for school plays, track and field, completion of schoolwork, and preparation for tests and quizzes there is no time for television.

47: listen to what they listen to

Music: My wife and I try as much as possible to listen to the lyrics within the music our sons listen to. Clearly, censorship is required to varying degrees for both of them. We do not allow either of them to listen to music through headphones when we are gathered together at home or in the car. Whatever music is being played, everyone listens to, subsequently, the music has to be appropriate for everyone to hear. The same applies to movies, both at the theater and on DVD.

48: do not let them surf alone

Internet: My wife and I eased the restrictions on our then, sixteen-year-old son in regards to Internet access and participation in Internet chat rooms. As a high school junior, he was a year away from college and subsequently our ability to monitor his Internet access. While we continued to limit access to Internet web sites and the time in Internet chat rooms, we constantly reaffirmed how a person's core values and beliefs should not be discarded behind the cloak of screen names and the anonymity of Internet users. Our older son did not have Internet access in his bedroom or behind a closed door in any room. Our younger son does not have any unsupervised Internet access and is not allowed to participate in chat room discussions.

49: utilize your influence

Adults exert direct influence by:

- having relationships with young people which provide frequent opportunities to share experiences, provide insight, and share stories which inspire hope and provide advice for dealing with issues and conflicts;

- establishing parameters in classrooms, households, and in school-related programs and activities that define an expected standard of behavior, acceptable methods of resolving conflicts, and the level of compassion to be directed toward others;

- being physically involved in activities and at events that may result in conflicts or inappropriate behaviors;

- consciously recognizing, rewarding, and validating a code of conduct and standard of behavior;

- being aware of the issues unique to your school community, e.g., sexual promiscuity, suicides, depression, anxiety disorders, gangs, drugs, bullying;

- spending quality time involved in the activities which are important to young men, e.g., sporting events, movies, concerts, parties, shopping, outdoor activities;

- taking advantage of long rides, vacations, or evenings together as opportunities to talk about issues of concern to young men or sharing hobbies and areas of interests;

- taking advantage of opportunities to exert direct influence by coordinating activities, planning events, or exposing young men to a wide range of opportunities;

- taking advantage of the opportunity to discuss music, fashion choices, hair styles, and the other cultural images; or
- taking advantage of opportunities to discuss current issues, topics being discussed at school, and issues emanating from popular culture.

50: influence their peer group

Adults exert influence through peers indirectly when they:

- identify those young men who are respected by peers and who model the type of values and level of achievement that you would like others to aspire toward and use them to inspire their friends;
- take seriously the responsibility of selecting young men as captains of athletic teams, officers in organizations, or project leaders in classrooms as an opportunity to identify and recognize those young people who embody the types of values and provide the types of examples you want to reinforce;

- provide opportunities for interaction with young Black males who have gone through some of the difficult choices confronting their respective age group, i.e., dealing with peer pressures, transitions from elementary to middle school, middle to high school, and high school to college;

- coordinate town-hall style meetings or discussion groups where young men have an opportunity to share and challenge each other's ideas and opinions;

- coordinate opportunities for cross-socioeconomic, cross-ethnic, and cross-gender discussion groups to stimulate discussions pertaining to academic goals, attitudes, dreams, aspirations, and current issues;

- identify clubs and organizations to involve young men in, e.g., NAACP, 100 Black Men, fraternities, Upward Bound, Jack and Jill, Masons, Boy Scouts, Boys & Girls Clubs, Big Brothers Big Sisters, after-school programs, summer programs and camps, mentoring, and leadership organizations;

- take advantage of opportunities for long rides to museums, plays, college campuses, concerts, and athletic events to listen to the thoughts, ideas, beliefs, values, and opinions of peers; or

- take a young man out of organizations or activities that do not reinforce positive values and high expectations and be aware of the time spent with peers in unsupervised activities.

51: expand the curriculum

Combating the negative influences received from the media and reinforced by peers requires:

1. Using the existing curriculum to teach and reinforce the needed lessons.

2. Identifying supplemental materials and programs (i.e., literature, stories, proverbs, guest speakers, field trips, writing, art, and oratorical competitions).

Use the curriculum to combat negative influences of media imagery and peer pressures by:

- identifying and recognizing facts as they relate to Black influence across subject areas, i.e., writers, poets, actors, actresses, scientists, inventors, explorers, educators, architects, political figures, entrepreneurs, and world leaders;

- identifying opportunities to demonstrate learning through multiple intelligences-related activities, i.e., constructing models, oral presentations, musical, dance, and theatrical performances, artistic renderings, plays, skits, role playing, raps, poetry, and videos;

- utilizing multiple intelligences-related activities to structure cooperative groups where students accept research and presentation responsibilities within their dominant areas of intelligence contributing to multi-media and multi-faceted group presentations;

- creating visual imagery through bulletin boards, walls, display cases, T-shirts, and posters, recognizing and reinforcing Black achievement to be displayed throughout the school and throughout the school year;

- creating visual displays of career themes relating specifically to areas of the curriculum which in essence answer the question, "Why do I need to know this?";

- utilizing opportunities to introduce young men to Black writers and literary figures in a conscious effort to wean them away from television and video games into reading and literary analysis;

- encouraging research in regards to Black historical figures for book reports and research papers;

- encouraging research in regards to Black historical figures within student interest areas, i.e., professional sports, entertainment, clothing manufacturers, hair stylists, artists, actors, and musicians; or

- encouraging students to tailor assignments to areas of interests or to areas of need (i.e., learning more about who they are, where they came from, and the historical achievements of Black people).

What Blacks are now being taught does not bring their minds into harmony with life as they must face it. When a Black student works his way through college by polishing shoes, he does not think of making a special study of the science underlying the production and distribution of leather and its products that he may some day figure in this sphere. The Black boy sent to college by a mechanic seldom dreams of learning mechanical engineering to build upon the foundation his father had laid, that in years to come he may figure as a contractor or consulting engineer.

— *Dr. Carter G. Woodson*

52: inspire academic rigor

As school districts throughout the country focus attention on the 3Rs (Rigor, Relevance, and Relationships), Black males are most often the least-likely students to be enrolled in academically rigorous classes. They rarely understand the relevance of academically rigorous course work or have the necessary relationship with teachers, counselors, and coaches to be encouraged toward, or gain full access into, the complete range of academic enrichment programs, academic clubs, or honors, pre-AP, and AP classes within any public school district. Despite a wide-spread belief that they are unmotivated, the fact is, neither the young men nor their families are likely to fully understand the complete scope of the opportunities within the school district and the potential impact such course work and programs can have on a young man's long-term dreams and aspirations.

To ensure that Black males are equitably represented in academically rigorous classes, enrichment programs, and academically-oriented clubs and activities, each school must gather its disaggregate data pertaining to Black male enrollment and performance. Once inequities are identified, teachers, counselors, coaches, and parents must work together to encourage and support full participation in such programs and activities.

- Ensure that each young man has a kindergarten-through-twelfth-grade course schedule based on his areas of interest, i.e., art, music, dance, science, math, athletics, computers, acting, or talking.

- Help each young man set up a subject-area binder for each class, each school year to contain the course syllabus, assignment log, monthly calendar, study sheets, and tabs (i.e., homework, notes, tests and quizzes, extra credit).

- Discuss or create a visual of how each class relates to his kindergarten-through-twelfth-grade plan.

- Create a parent information sheet that outlines what parents can do to assist students in achieving the highest grade in your class and establish a preferred home-school communication method.

53: provide guidance & support

- Tell students/families at the beginning of the grading period what they will be expected to know at the end of the grading period.
- Clarify the standards in parent-friendly language.
- Create at-home tips (refrigerator sheets) to reinforce content areas.
- Ensure that unit tests, quizzes, and exams are aligned with the standards, reinforce problem-solving approaches, and reinforce testing language (i.e., contrast, compare, and most likely).
- Identify student incentives (i.e., grading methodology, make-up policy, and extra credit opportunities) to tap students' intrinsic motivation.
- Provide students and parents with clear grading rubrics for major projects and assignments that are written in parent-friendly language. Grading rubrics should provide examples of quality work and clear step-by-step instructions of how to successfully meet your expectations.

The importance of reading literacy, fluency, and an appreciation of books and published literature cannot be underestimated or compromised. The current school, community, church, and household influences of Black male literacy simply do not do enough to encourage reading and reading literacy. Black males are more likely to have a collection of video games rather than a collection of books, and they are more likely to receive a video game from an adult as a gift than they are to receive a book!

Lack of reading fluency and proficiency is a clear predictor of future incarceration. A popular, yet unproven, Internet story suggests that third grade reading scores are used to predict the number of prison beds that will be needed in the future. Whether or not there is any validity to this story, research does show the majority of the state and federal prison inmates lack high levels of literacy, many of whom are functionally illiterate.

54: reinforce reading

In *Reading for Change: Performance and Engagement Across Countries,* published by the Organization for Economic Co-Operation and Development (OECD), it is noted:

> *Lewis (2002) claims that some states in the United States use third-grade reading statistics to determine how many prison beds they will need in 10 years' time. Though this might seem far-fetched, it has been reported that half of all adults in U.S. federal prisons cannot read or write at all. The typical 25-year-old male inmate functions two or three grade levels below the grade actually completed (Bellarado, 1986).*

The doorway to opportunity is opening and closing every moment throughout our lifetime. However, each time that the door of opportunity opens, there are a lot of other people trying to go through before the door closes. That's called "competition," a fact of life. Take it or leave it, like it or lump it, that's just the way it is. Whether a football game or Spelling Bee, a college application or a job application, a Science Fair or a Track Meet, a cheerleading tryout or a band audition, throughout your lifetime you are going to be confronted with competition for each opportunity.

The greatest obstacle to anyone's success is KNOWLEDGE—plain and simple. Regardless of what color you are, how poor you are, where you were born, where you live, what you look like, whether or not your mama helps you with your homework, whether or not you have a computer at home or whether or not you even have a home to go to, expand your knowledge and you will expand your opportunity. If you know little, then you can achieve little. If you know a lot, then you can achieve a lot. The question is, "You got game?"

[Follow Your Dreams: Lessons That I Learned in School, p. 13]

Chapter 5

Instruction

Expectations

Nowhere is there a greater misunderstanding, miscommunication, and conflict between Black parents and classroom teachers than as it relates to the education of Black children. Black parents want to see their children succeed academically, however, they are less likely than White parents to have a positive relationship with classroom teachers to ensure that this happens. Without such a relationship, predictable problems, such as: lack of organization; ineffective note taking; late assignments; poor test preparation; and lack of preexisting knowledge, are rarely addressed (at least to the satisfaction of Black parents). Subsequently, parents become increasingly frustrated and develop negative attitudes toward schools and classroom teachers.

55: parent-teacher collaboration

Building the bridge between parents and teachers so they are talking about what to do to ensure that Black children are successful academically will do more to close the achievement gap and increase the societal success of Black children in general, and Black males in particular, than perhaps any other single initiative. Building such a bridge begins with understanding the roadblocks between teachers and Black parents and conceptualizing strategies to develop more effective communication and build stronger relationships. In so doing, teachers must keep in mind, as previously outlined in Chapter three, *Climate and Culture*, the communication and relationship may not be with a student's parents but with another influential adult, i.e., aunt, uncle, grandparent, older sibling, coach, pastor, or mentor.

56: grading methodology

Grading methodology and grading practices must be constructed in ways that are student and parent-friendly. Grades not only provide an assessment mechanism but also should provide a *motivating factor* in encouraging student effort as students set and pursue their own goals. Grading policies should take into account student needs, developmental levels, student interests, and the overall goal—learning. Michael Gurian, in *Boys and Girls Learn Differently*, notes such grading disparities as:

- Girls receive approximately 60 percent of the A's.
- Boys receive approximately 70 percent of the D's and F's.
- Girls account for 63 percent of students performing in the top 20 percent of high school grade ranges.
- Boys account for 90 percent of the discipline problems and 80 percent of dropouts.

57: encourage risk taking

Alphie Kohn, in *Punished by Rewards*, notes the importance of structuring an environment in which students can explore, make mistakes, acknowledge when they do not know, and risk failing without risk of ridicule from the teacher or their peers:

> ... *a classroom that feels safe to students is one in which they are free to admit when they don't understand something and are able to ask for help. Ironically, grades and tests, punishments and rewards, are the enemies of safety; they therefore reduce the probability that students will speak up and that truly productive evaluation can take place.*

> ... *just as adults who love their work will invariably do a better job than those goaded with artificial incentives, so children are more likely to be optimal learners if they are interested in what they are learning.*

58: look for their gifts

When young men exhibit their extraordinary energy levels it is considered a deficiency in the classroom and they are labeled as hyperactive. The same energy and intensity on the football field or basketball court is valued and they are received throughout the school and community as heroes. When they speak loudly and play roughly at school they are labeled as wild and coming from poor home environments. Outside of the school they are signed to contracts in professional wrestling, produce CDs, and receive leading roles in plays.

Avoid labels and identify opportunities to apply their abilities, expand their gifts, harness their energy, help them to value their uniqueness and affirm their dreams.

59: facilitate bonding

- Shake students hands as they enter the classroom.

- Touch a student's shoulder or slap a student on the back when he participates in a classroom discussion.

- Address students by their surname, i.e., Mr. Wynn, Mr. Kambon, Mr. Carreker, Mr. Jones, or Mr. McBride.

- Be consistent.

- Set clear expectations, rules, and procedures.

- Avoid confrontations and step outside of the classroom with students who are determined to engage in a confrontation.

- Get to know each student's family.

- Create a risk-free environment, i.e., no laughing, name-calling, or put-downs.

- Never threaten a student!

Chapter 6

Assessment

Black males, at each grade level, will be assessed on varying formal assessment mechanisms, i.e., EOCT, EOG, standardized testing, state mandated testing, high school exit exams, SAT, ACT, PSAT, etc. Their performance is assessed and readily available. However, if we revisit the discussion in the *Overview*, "What is the problem?" there are many more areas, not formally assessed by the school, which must be assessed if we are to move toward the necessary solutions to the Black male achievement crisis—lack of parental involvement, under representation in gifted, honors, and AP classes, late entry into the algebra I and foreign language pipelines, and the disparity between prison incarceration and college matriculation.

60: do not make assumptions

Avoid making assumptions and engage in deliberate analysis of the factors influencing Black male achievement—both academically and socially. The contributing factors to student achievement are usually much more than teacher effectiveness or student ability—classroom structure, at-home support, extracurricular activity involvement, culturally relevant pedagogy, teaching styles, learning styles, student levels of preexisting knowledge and involvement in study groups are but some of the many factors that must be identified and assessed.

Such analysis will involve raising such questions as:

- What is the teacher's dominant teaching style?
- What is the student's dominant learning style?

- How would you describe the student's access to academic support (i.e., study groups, before- and after-school tutoring, at-home support, older siblings, resource and supplemental materials, etc.)?

- What is the student's level of preexisting knowledge, higher-order thinking, or critical-thinking skills?

- Does the student demonstrate effective study, note-taking, and test preparation skills?

- Is the student experiencing difficulty balancing academic preparation, extracurricular activity involvement, or after-school responsibilities?

61: assess parent attitudes

In most school communities there is a clear lack of Black parental involvement. To more fully assess this lack of parental involvement, consider the following questions:

- Is academic achievement a parental priority?

- What level of educational achievement have parents attained and what level of achievement is envisioned for their children?
- How would parents describe their experiences as a student?
- How would parents describe their experiences with teachers in previous classes or grade levels?
- What are the home and work demands on parents (i.e., how many children, employment demands, available home and community support)?
- What personal issues hinder parental involvement (e.g., health, self-esteem, criminal backgrounds, or discomfort with being in a school setting)?

62: assess classroom practices

- Are there identifiable instructional gaps (e.g., cross-generational, cross-gender, cross-cultural, cross-socio-economic, teaching—learning-style, etc.)?
- Are students actively engaged and does the teacher maximize time-on-task?

- Are classroom seating arrangements conducive to reducing personal conflicts and enhancing learning?
- Are classroom management strategies appropriate and timely in preventing or reducing conflicts?
- Are progress reports and parent communication effectively used as intervention tools to enhance student learning?
- Is cooperative grouping being effectively used to enhance student learning and to create a classroom climate of shared ownership for student success?

63: be patient and encouraging

Useni Eugene Perkins, in *Harvesting New Generations: The Positive Development of Black Youth,* quotes Booker T. Washington:

"The world should not pass judgment upon the Negro, and especially upon the Negro youth, too quickly or too harshly. The Negro boy has obstacles, discouragements, and temptations to battle with that are little known to those not situated as he is.

When a white boy undertakes a task, it is taken for granted that he will succeed. On the other hand, people are usually surprised if the Negro boy does not fail. In a word, the Negro youth starts out with the presumption against him."

With the deck already stacked against Black males, we cannot allow anyone (including parents) to discourage them from setting extraordinary goals for themselves. Even the young man who has never received an 'A' on his report card must be considered an 'A' student on the first day of class.

"Class, on your desks you will find a paper with today's grade on it. Please place it into your binder and take it home to your parents. If your parents sign it and let me know the best way to get in touch with them in the event I need their help in ensuring you remain 'A' students it will count as your first extra credit grade."

A little boy walks up to the teacher. "Excuse me sir. You must have made a mistake. I ain't never been no 'A' student."

The teacher corrects the little boy's use of non-Standard English.

"I haven't received an 'A' before." The little boy responds, "You neither?"

The teacher goes on to explain to the little boy, "Young man, I'm an 'A' teacher and everyone in this classroom is an 'A' student. Since everyone is here today to learn, every one of my students, including you, is an 'A' student today. If each student does what is expected of he or she throughout the balance of the grading period, then every student will be an 'A' student on the final day of the grading period as well. If you are not an 'A' student, then in some way I would have failed you as your teacher and I don't like to fail at anything."

The little boy stares at the teacher in disbelief. "Sir, if you're an 'A' teacher and I'm an 'A' student, then would you please call my mama after school today? She just isn't going to believe this. I just ain't never been no 'A', oh excuse me, I have never been an 'A' student before."

64: follow your compass

What is in the best interest of the child?

Using this simple standard as the compass to guide the way, parents and teachers, can continually assess, evaluate, and challenge preexisting ideas and beliefs. Rules, consequences, rewards, and extrinsically motivating factors and strategies should undergo continual discussion, debate, adjustment, implementation, assessment, and reevaluation. This is not to suggest Black males be held to impossibly high standards. It is the continuing discussions and analysis which must be engaged in, always keeping in mind a future focus, "What type of men, husbands, fathers, employees, or entrepreneurs are we attempting to develop?"

Possible courses of action for classroom teachers:

- Allow frequent opportunities to redo work, resubmit homework and projects, and retake tests and quizzes to encourage continuing review of course content, deepening of knowledge, and the opportunity for before- after-school or tutorial support to inspire continually reaching for higher grades, and subsequently, higher levels of learning.

- Establish "Homework Make-up and Retesting Days" where students have the opportunity to make up work, retake tests and quizzes, and demonstrate content knowledge.

- Develop communication and shared expectations with parents, coaches, tutors, or mentors to ensure completion of class work, submission of homework, preparation for tests, and classroom participation.

- Review grading methodology, homework policy, and policy for retaking tests within the simple context of, "Is this in the best interest of students?"

- Give students ownership of their own assessment by using effective grading rubrics, encouraging students to set their own goals, track their own progress, and take ownership of their own success.

65: make learning a priority

Possible courses of action for parents or mentors:

- Meet with teachers to discuss the aforementioned ideas with the goal of developing common expectations and appropriate strategies that will nurture academic effort and encourage academic excellence.

- When your son falls behind in his schoolwork he may need to sacrifice his weekend to catch up. Despite his unwillingness to sacrifice 'his' time to catch up on 'his business' what you do will have long-range consequences and clearly communicate your expectations, or lack thereof, as it pertains to academic excellence.

Following are some of the strategies my wife and I have utilized to reinforce our expectations:

- Unplug and pack away (very ceremoniously) video game systems at the beginning of the school year and we leave them packed away until the holiday or end of the school year.

- Take all of the designer clothes and shoes out of our older son's closet until after the first progress report grades come home. He is able to use some of his grades to buy back articles of clothing.

- No weekend activities until all homework and projects are completed. The one exception is if they are up-to-date in all of their classes, they are able to participate in team sports where teammates depend on their contribution.

- No television from Sunday evening through Thursday evening unless they are up-to-date in every class, have all homework and projects completed, do not have any late assignments, and have completed all of their chores (as you may guess, they rarely earn the right to watch television during the week).

- Each of our sons begins the school year with a box containing everything required to successfully complete homework, i.e., dictionary, thesaurus, ruler, pens, pencils, pencil sharpener, three-hole-puncher, paper, colored pencils, and highlight markers.

- No telephone calls until all schoolwork and homework have been completed.

- E-mail teachers regularly (sometimes daily) and monitor their grades throughout the grading period.
- Post report cards and standardized test scores onto the refrigerator for everyone to see and to provide continuing reinforcement of high expectations.

Freeman Hrabowski, president of the University of Maryland Baltimore County, in *Beating the Odds: Raising Academically Successful African American Males*, notes:

> *In our work, we often hear African American parents expressing the hope and desire that their children will achieve at the highest levels academically. What we also hear from these parents, though, is that one rarely sees in the media examples of young Black males who are achieving academically, being rewarded for those achievements, and feeling good about being smart. Even among advantaged African American families, we find that young males are heavily influenced by the popular culture that discourages pride in high academic achievement, demands that young Black males present a hard veneer to the world, and provides numerous opportunities for these young males to become involved in a world of crime and drugs. In fact, the idea of this book originated from our concern about the frightening status of young African American males and the need to find effective, family-based, educational solutions to enhance their futures.*

66: assess academic success

The ability for parents and teachers to reach agreement as to strategies and expectations is critical to the continuing academic success of Black males. These strategies must take into account the lack of academic support among peers, school-wide cultures that do not promote or reinforce academic achievement, and any prior history of low teacher or parent expectations.

We do not help young men by allowing them to develop poor study habits, low personal academic expectations, and dwell at the bottom of the academic achievement gap. When schools have academic recognition days, honor roll ceremonies, induction into the National Honor Society or Beta Club and there is a noticeable absence of Black males, we eventually find it is less noticeable that they are not participating as the entire school community comes to expect their absence.

Epilogue

Turn the Ships Around

Pearl Cleage, in her book *Deals with the Devil and Other Reasons to Riot*, describes the communication breakdown between Black women and Black men in dealing with some of the pressing issues of the Black community, families, and the rearing of Black children.

> *Brothers feel that we, their sisters, are giving mixed signals when it comes to the manhood thing. We want, they say, all the protection and safety offered by a strong man, but we are unwilling to accept the presence of the warrior's heart.*

> *We, they say, are responsible for any confusion that exists on the manhood question; we are the ones, they say, that counsel caution instead of courage; diplomacy instead of defense.*

They say that when the ships pulled up on the shores of Africa and slavers came ashore to look for us, we were the ones who held them back; the ones who told them that it might be dangerous to go down to the water's edge.

We were the ones, they say, who encouraged them to stay at home, telling them how worried we would be if they went down there with the other warriors to turn the ships around, assuring them that if they just sat here by the fire with us, the white folks would probably change their minds and go away all by themselves.

They say that's the reason why they didn't turn the ships around. Because they thought we didn't want them to.

It has been my intent in writing the book upon which this book has been taken *[Empowering African-American Males to Succeed: A Guide to Increasing Black Male Achievement]* to provide clear strategies and solutions to many of the issues hindering the education of Black males. Turning the ships around will require that we, as champions for Black males (i.e., parents, teachers, coaches, mentors, principals and preachers), develop the courage to turn the ships around.

What Manner of Men are We ...

Who move fluidly and swiftly
    along the football fields
    and basketball courts of the world
Constantly pounding or being pounded
In the boxing rings
    of Atlantic City and the inner city
Robbed from the bosom
    of Mother Africa
    the richness of South Africa
Having journeyed from the mountain top
    to the selling block
Withstanding over 300 years
    of castration and degradation,
Experiencing every indignity and humiliation
Yet continuing to grow tall and strong
Creating a history rich in achievement
We discovered blood plasma
    and the cotton gin
Gas masks and harpoons

      baby carriages and traffic lights
Machines to plant seeds
      and machines to stretch shoes
We were the first to die
      in the struggle for
      this country's independence
And the first to successfully
      perform open heart surgery
We are Martin and Marcus, Malcolm and Benjamin
Frederick and W.E.B., Jesse and Booker T.
We are Jesse, Jackie, and Joe
      the Big E, and the Big O
We are Clyde the Glide and Earl the Pearl
We are the Watusi and the Mandingo
There are none bigger,
      none better,
      none taller,
      none stronger,
Than we, when we have it all together
That's what manner of men we are

– Mychal Wynn

References

The content of this book has been excerpted entirely from the book, *Empowering African-American Males: A Guide to Increasing Black Male Achievement*. Please refer to the larger text for the complete references and research studies. Refer to the *Empowering African-American Males: Teaching, Parenting, and Mentoring Successful Black Males workbook* for a comprehensive listing of activities to inspire Black male achievement.

Wynn, Mychal. (2005). *Empowering African-American Males: A Guide to Increasing Black Male Achievement*. Marietta, GA: Rising Sun Publishing.

For ordering information, contact:

Rising Sun Publishing
P.O. Box 70906
Marietta, GA 30007
Phone: (770) 518-0369
FAX: (770) 587-0862
Web site: www.rspublishing.com
E-mail: info@rspublishing.com

Index

A

Framework For Understanding Poverty, 55
High School Plan for Students with College-Bound Dreams, 98
Abu Simbel, 2
Accra, Ghana, 2
ACT, 6, 20, 98
Africa, 2, 113
Africans, 51-52
Air Force, 18
Akbar, Na'im, 65
Alabama, vii, 2
Amherst College, viii
AP, 6, 20, 98
Armed Forces, 18

Beating The Odds, 110
Beliefs, 19-20, 43, 79, 83, 105
Beta Club, 111
Beyond Identify, 66
Big Brothers Big Sisters, 83
Black-White Inequality, 4
Boy Scouts, 83

Cairo, Egypt, 2

Carter, Ken, 23-25
Clark, Joe, 23
Cleage, Pearl, 112
Coach Carter, 23-25
Cochran, Johnnie, 28
Coaching, 11, 38
Crenshaw Christian Center, 52

Department of Education, 31-32, 60
Deals with the Devil, 112

Ebonics, 72
Edmonds, Ron, x
Effective Schools, 13
Egyptian Museum, 2
Empowering African-American Males, iv-v, viii-ix, 1, 3, 16, 73, 112, 114
English, 6, 44, 50, 53, 69-70, 104
Ephesians, 51

FUBU, 34
Follow Your Dreams, 91
Future Role of Black Americans, 66

Gary, Willie, 28
GED, 91
Gender, 55, 59, 61, 72
Generational, 54, 59, 61
George McKenna Story, 23

Ghana, 2
Ghanaians, 3
Girls Clubs, 83
Giza, Egypt, 2
Glionna, John M., 25
Gurian, Michael, 59, 94

Hale-Benson, Janice 61
Harvesting New Generations, 102
HBCUs, 27
Henderson, George, 67
Hidden Rules, 55
Hispanic, 5-6
Historically Black Colleges, 27
Homework Make-up and Retesting Days, 106
Howard University, 34
Hrabowski, Freeman, 110

Internet, 46-47, 79-80, 90
It Takes A Village, 8
Jack and Jill, 83

Kohn, Alphie, 95
Kunjufu, Jawanza, 57
Kuykendall, Crystal 57

Lean on Me, 23
Learning-styles, 9, 21, 42, 61, 99

Los Angeles Times, 25
Luxor, Egypt, 2
Lying Lewis, 57-58

Malcolm X, 44
Men are from Venus and Women are from Mars, 55
Marshall, Thurgood 28
Marva Collins Story, 23
Masons, 83
Mathematics Equals Opportunity, 32
Military Academy, 18
Mission Statements, 13
Multiple Intelligences, 21, 42

National
    Bar Association, 28
    Education Longitudinal Study, 32
    Honor Society, 111
NBA, 34
Negro, 29, 102-103
New Jersey, 58
Newark, 58
NFL, 34
Nile, 2
Non-Standard English, 53, 104
Nubian, 2

OECD, 90

P. Diddy, 34
Palm Beach County Florida, 29
Payne, Ruby, 55
Perkins, Useni Eugene, 102
Phat Farm, 34
Pike County, vii
Positive Development of Black Youth, 102
Price, Frederick K. C. 52
Punished by Rewards, 95

Raising Academically Successful African American Males, 110
Reading for Change: Performance and Engagement Across Countries, 90
Reinforce Standard English, 50, 53, 69
Richmond High School, 23, 25
Roxbury, 44

Sahara, 2
San Francisco, 25
SAT, 98
Sean John, 34
Shaw University, 28
Special Education, 4-5
Spiritual, 8-9, 52, 65
Standard English, 50, 53, 69-70

Successful Texas School-wide Programs, 13
Tatum, Beverly Daniel, 44
Television Programming, 47, 50, 78
Ten Steps to Helping Your Child Succeed in School, 63
The
  Autobiography of Malcolm X, 44
  Conspiracy to Destroy Black Boys, 57
  Eagles who Thought They were Chickens, 51
  Mis-Education of the Negro, 29
  Tom Joyner Morning Show, 48

U. S.
  Census Bureau, 3
  Department of Education, 31-32
University of Maryland Baltimore County, 110
Upward Bound, 83

Washington, Booker T., 102
Weaver, Ron, 66
What manner of men are we, 113
Wholistic Institute, 57
Why Are All the Black Children Sitting Together in the Cafeteria, 44
Woodson, Carter G., 29, 35